SINEAD O'CONNOR:

Unraveling the Soul of a Fearless Artist

(8 December 1966 – 26 July 2023)

Mary D. Durgan

Sinéad O'Connor

TABLE OF CONTENTS

INTRODUCTION

Only a select few musicians throughout the history of music have ventured to expose their souls in this way, and Sinead O'Connor stands out among them. She has had an enduring impact on the music industry and beyond with a voice that taps into the depths of human emotion and a spirit that won't be silenced. We set out on a mission to comprehend the lady behind the music, the conflicts, and the unwavering commitment to her values in this investigation of her life and career.

We go into Sinead O'Connor's riveting story chapter by chapter, tracing the origins of her unrivaled talent and the significant influence she has had on the world. Sinead's early years were full of difficulties that shaped her artistic expression and uncompromising devotion to authenticity because she was born into a life that defied convention.

Sinéad O'Connor

Her poor beginnings in Ireland, a country with a long history of independence fights and rich cultural traditions, are described in Chapter 1. Sinead's strong connection to her Irish heritage would influence her music from an early age and serve as a powerful source of inspiration for the rest of her career.

Her artistic development is examined in Chapter 2, starting with her early involvement in local bands and ending with the publication of her debut album, "The Lion and the Cobra." We see the emergence of a remarkable talent and the entry of a fresh voice into the music business. Audiences were enthralled by Sinead's raw, sensitive, and hauntingly beautiful voice, which won her praise and made her a force to be reckoned with.

However, celebrity often brings scrutiny, and Chapter 3 explores the squabbles that Sinead faced throughout her career. She never shied away from questioning society norms and criticizing the current quo, from the infamous SNL Pope photo incident to her outspoken views on politics and religion. We look at how her bold expression had an impact on both her personal and professional life.

In Chapter 4, Sinead's difficulties with mental health and how they affected her music are explored in more detail. As she struggled with depression and bipolar disease, she found comfort and power in her work, creating songs that served as a window into her inner turmoil as well as a ray of light for countless followers going through similar struggles.

Chapter 5 focuses on her partnerships and contributions outside of her solo work. We see how Sinead's ability stretched beyond her own records, leaving an enduring effect on the larger musical world, from legendary duets with other performers to her composing for others.

Chapter 6 is devoted to the honors and accolades she has received, commemorating the industry and scholarly acknowledgement of her extraordinary talent. Sinead's true legacy, however, is found in the significant effect she had on the music industry and the lives of individuals who sought comfort and motivation in her songs.

The last chapter examines Sinead O'Connor's continued career and most recent developments. Her music has developed throughout the years, and her live performances are still as compelling and forceful as ever.

We develop a tremendous respect for the soul of a daring artist throughout this trip. The life and work of Sinead O'Connor serve as a shining example of the unifying, healing, and elevating effects that music can have on people. Come celebrate Sinead O'Connor's life, challenges, and incredible musical legacy with us.

CHAPTER 1: EARLY YEARS AND BACKGROUND

On December 8, 1966, Sinead O'Connor was born in the Dublin, Ireland neighborhood of Glenageary. She was the third kid in a family of five that would experience many difficulties. The early divorce of her parents, John and Marie O'Connor, had a significant impact on her upbringing.

As a child growing up in Ireland in the 1970s and 1980s, Sinead was exposed to a culture riven with racial and political divisions. The Troubles, a period of bloody hostility between Catholics and Protestants in Northern Ireland, were a problem for the nation. Her activism and music would subsequently be influenced by this milieu, and she frequently utilized her platform to speak out against social and political issues, particularly those connected to her Roman Catholic upbringing.

Sinéad O'Connor

Sinead showed a deep passion for music at a young age, as well as musical skill. She started singing in the community church choir, where she fell in love with the arts and artistic expression. Despite her financial struggles, she was able to enroll in a convent school where she sharpened her musical abilities and found her distinctive voice.

Sinead's life experienced turmoil when she was committed to a Magdalene Asylum, a Catholic facility for "wayward" girls, as a result of being discovered shoplifting during her adolescence. She later confessed that this encounter had a lasting effect on her because it had left emotional and psychological wounds. Despite the difficulties, Sinead persisted in pursuing her love of music.

Sinead entered the Dublin music scene in her late teens and played in a number of regional bands. She got significant expertise during this time and started to create her distinctive sound and style. Her distinctively shaven head became an iconic visual emblem connected with her image, frequently perceived as a striking act of defiance against conventional standards.

Sinead's upbringing and history helped to create the artist she is today—one who unapologetically embraces her uniqueness and defies social norms. Themes and messages weaved throughout her songs were significantly shaped by her Irish ethnicity, her complicated upbringing, and her experiences inside the Catholic Church.

Sinead O'Connor's songs evolved into a platform for her to express her social justice passion, convictions, and personal hardships as her career took off and she received widespread acclaim. We will explore further into her incredible career as a singer, activist, and significant person in the music industry in the chapters that will come.

1.1 Musical Impact

The musical tastes of Sinead O'Connor are as varied and broad as her own collection of work. She has absorbed influences from a variety of genres and artists over the course of her career, helping to create her own style and advance her artistic development. The following are some of the major musical inspirations that Sinead O'Connor has drawn from:

1. Irish Folk Music: Sinead was exposed to traditional Irish folk music at a young age while growing up in Ireland. This genre's deep storytelling and emotional depth had a significant influence on her music. Many of her songs have Irish folk elements, which give her music a distinctively Celtic feel.

2. Soul and R&B: Sinead has named Sam Cooke, Otis Redding, and Marvin Gaye as important influences on her musical career. Her own powerful and emotionally charged vocal performances were inspired by the soulful and expressive vocal stylings of these musicians.

3. Reggae: Sinead's love in this genre of music can be heard in several of her later compositions, particularly her 2005 album "Throw Down Your Arms." Her affinity for reggae and its socially aware ideas are evident in this album's assortment of reggae covers.

4. Punk and New Wave: Sinead was exposed to the drive and DIY attitude of punk and new wave music during her formative years in the Dublin music scene. Her debut album, "The Lion and the Cobra," which included punk-inspired sounds, reflects how both genres affected her early artistic expression.

5. Gospel and Spiritual Music: Sinead was exposed to gospel and spiritual music during her youth in the Catholic Church, and this experience had a lasting impact on her. Many of her compositions, which are reflections of her own challenges and spiritual journey, have the soul-stirring power of gospel choirs and the profundity of spiritual issues.

6. Rock and Alternative Music: As her career developed, Sinead delved more into the rock and alternative genre, as evidenced by the inclusion of these genres in albums like "I Do Not Want What I Haven't Got" and "Universal Mother." She draws inspiration from Jimi Hendrix and Bob Dylan, among other rock legends, in both her lyrics and instrumental arrangements.

7. Classical Music: In several of her pieces, Sinead shows her passion for classical music by including orchestral arrangements and melodic structures that were influenced by classical composers.

8. Bob Marley: Sinead frequently gushed about how much she admired the great reggae artist Bob Marley, both as a musical icon and a social activist. Her personal ideas and ideals were in line with his messages of love, harmony, and justice.

The combination of these various musical influences helped give Sinead O'Connor her distinctive and potent voice. She has cemented her position as one of the most influential and genuine musicians in the history of current music with her ability to adroitly meld several genres and infuse her music with raw emotion and social commentary.

1.2 Rise to Fame

Sinead O'Connor's meteoric rise to popularity was defined by talent, tenacity, and a voice that won over listeners all over the world. The following is a summary of her journey to becoming a widely recognized artist:

1. Early Dublin Performances: Sinead O'Connor launched her musical career in the thriving Dublin music scene in the early 1980s. She joined neighborhood bands and developed valuable live performance experience while exhibiting her strong voice and distinctive stage presence. Insiders in the music industry and music aficionados alike were soon drawn to her talent.

2. First release: "The Lion and the Cobra" (1987):

Sinéad O'Connor

The 1987 publication of Sinead's debut album, "The Lion and the Cobra," marked the start of her career. She gained international recognition for her distinctive voice and songwriting thanks to the album, which received favorable reviews. The lead song, "Mandinka," gained a lot of radio play and helped bring her to public attention.

3. Breakout Single: "Nothing Compares 2 U" Sinead's hauntingly moving performance of the Prince song "Nothing Compares 2 U" is largely responsible for her meteoric rise to fame. The main single from her second album, "I Do Not Want What I Haven't Got," was released in 1990. The song quickly rose to the top of the charts worldwide. She gained even more notoriety because to the music video that featured her recognizable bald head and unvarnished vulnerability.

4. Grammy popularity: Following the enormous popularity of "Nothing Compares 2 U," Sinead O'Connor received recognition with several Grammy nominations, including one for Record of the Year. She didn't take home the prize in that category, but she did for the song

Sinéad O'Connor

"I Do Not Want What I Haven't Got," solidifying her position as a trailblazing alternative musician.

5. Ongoing artistic development: Sinead O'Connor continued to put out well-received albums in the 1990s and the early 2000s, each of which showed off her development as an artist and desire to venture into uncharted musical waters. She further cemented her image as a varied and significant performer with albums like "Am I Not Your Girl?" (1992), "Universal Mother" (1994), and "Faith and Courage" (2000).

6. Disputations and Activism: Sinead's outspokenness and readiness to speak out on social and political problems helped her become well-known. She gained extra media attention and cemented her reputation as an artist unafraid to use her platform for activism as a result of her involvement in a number of incidents, including the SNL Pope photo incident and her protests against child abuse in the Catholic Church.

7. Legacy and Persistent Influence: Sinead O'Connor's influence on popular music and culture goes well beyond her initial notoriety. Artists and activists alike continue to be inspired by her voice, sincerity, and boldness. She has established herself as a legendary character in the history of popular music thanks to her contributions to the genre and willingness to tackle taboo themes.

Sinead O'Connor is still regarded as a significant and respected musician today, and audiences of all ages continue to be moved by the lasting impact of her pioneering work in the music industry. Her rise to fame from the Dublin music scene to the global stage is proof of the enduring power of artistic skill, passion, and indomitable spirit.

CHAPTER 2: DISCOGRAPHY

The career of Sinead O'Connor spans several decades and consists of a wide variety of albums, singles, and group projects. Her notable studio albums are listed below:

1. 1987's "The Lion and the Cobra"
- The songs "Troy," "Mandinka," and "I Want Your (Hands on Me)" are noteworthy.

2. "I Do Not Want What I Haven't Got" was released in 1990.
- Standout Songs: "The Emperor's New Clothes," "Nothing Compares 2 U," and "Three Babies"

3. (1992) "Am I Not Your Girl?"
- Standout Songs Include "Success Has Made a Failure of Our Home," "Don't Cry for Me Argentina," and "Black Coffee"

4. (1994) "Universal Mother"

- "Fire on Babylon," "Famine," and "All Babies" are notable tracks.

5. (2000)'s "Faith and Courage"

- The songs "No Man's Woman," "Jealous," and "Daddy I'm Fine" are noteworthy.

6. (2002)'s "Sean-Nós Nua"

- The songs "Peggy Gordon," "Molly Malone," and "My Lagan Love" are noteworthy.

7. 2005's "Throw Down Your Arms"

- "Jah Nuh Dead," "Curly Locks," and "Vampire" are notable songs.

8. (2007) "Theology"

"Something Beautiful," "I Don't Know How to Love Him," and "Out of the Depths" are notable songs.

9. (2012)'s "How About I Be Me (and You Be You)?"

Sinéad O'Connor

- The songs "4th and Vine," "Take Off Your Shoes," and "Reason with Me" are noteworthy.

In addition to her studio albums, Sinead O'Connor has made significant contributions to the works of other musicians through important collaborations. She received considerable praise for her work with The The on the song "Kingdom of Rain" off their album "Mind Bomb" (1989). She also worked with musicians like Massive Attack, Peter Gabriel, and Shane MacGowan, demonstrating her flexibility as a guest vocalist.

Sinead O'Connor has always placed a high value on her live performances, and she has recorded multiple live albums that perfectly capture the intensity and feeling of her performances. "Live at the Hammersmith Apollo" (2002) and "Goodnight, Thank You. You've Been a Lovely Audience" (2003) are a couple of her live releases.

The influence Sinead O'Connor has as a songwriter goes beyond just her own work. Her songs have been performed by other singers as a tribute to her potent compositions and moving lyrics. Prince, an American singer-songwriter, gave one of the most well-known renditions of her song "Nothing Compares 2 U." Prince is the author of the song.

Sinead O'Connor's music has frequently been characterized throughout her discography by its emotional depth, thought-provoking themes, and potent vocals. She bravely discusses social issues, personal hardships, and things of the heart, forging an enduring bond with her audience.

In addition to her music, Sinead O'Connor's record is distinguished by her unrelenting dedication to using her craft as a platform for social activism and supporting causes that are important to her. Generations of fans have been motivated by her lyrics to embrace their own authenticity and speak up for what they believe in. Her songs have served as anthems for empowerment, love, and justice.

Sinead O'Connor's discography has stood the test of time and is evidence of her continuing influence on the music business. Her position as a popular and respected figure in modern music has been solidified by her extraordinary talent, sincerity, and willingness to challenge social norms.

Sinead O'Connor's career is a monument to the ability of music to cross boundaries, touch souls, and effect long-lasting change in the world. With each new release, Sinead O'Connor continues to leave an enduring impression on her listeners' hearts. Her voice, which has remained emotive and current throughout the shaping of her musical legacy, has cemented her place as an icon in the pantheon of musical genius.

2.1 Group projects and solo songs

Sinead O'Connor has worked with a variety of other musicians during her career and has created a number of noteworthy singles that highlight her vocal diversity and openness to experimenting with diverse musical genres. Here are some of her well-known group projects and singles:

Collaborations:

1. "Kingdom of Rain" (with The The) is a song that was featured on the band's 1989 album "Mind Bomb" and showcased Sinead's mesmerizing voice in addition to the band's moody and atmospheric atmosphere.

2. "Haunted" (featuring Shane MacGowan) is a chilling duet that Sinead co-wrote with Shane MacGowan, lead singer of The Pogues. The tune, which was released in 1995, featured their powerful vocal performances.

3. "I'm Not Your Baby" (with U2) - This joint effort with renowned rock group U2 was released on their "Pop" album in 1997. Together with Bono's vocals, Sinead's were incorporated in the song, forming a potent duet.

4. "Special Cases" (co-written by Sinead and Massive Attack) is a track from the 2003 album "100th Window" by Massive Attack that features Sinead's ethereal vocals. Her unusual voice was mixed with the band's distinctive trip-hop sound in this collaboration.

5. "Guide Me God" (with Ghostland) - Ghostland's "Interview with the Angel" (2004) CD contains this song they wrote together. The electronic music gained a somber and reflective quality from Sinead's vocals.

6. "The Wolf is Getting Married" (with Ry Cooder) - Sinead and legendary guitarist Ry Cooder teamed up to create this enthralling song, which was published in 2011. Their musical genres came together flawlessly throughout the song.

Singles:

1. In 1990, Sinead's legendary performance of the Prince song "Nothing Compares 2 U" served as her

breakthrough record and catapulted her to international stardom.

2. From her debut album, "The Lion and the Cobra," came the eerie and potent track "Troy" (1987), which gave Sinead's vocal range and ferocity a chance to shine.

3. Another outstanding song from "I Do Not Want What I Haven't Got," "The Emperor's New Clothes" (1990) is notable for its thought-provoking lyrics and engaging vocal delivery.

4. "Mandinka" (1987) – The lead song from Sinead O'Connor's debut album, "Mandinka," helped a larger audience become familiar with her distinctive sound and appearance.

5. A very vulnerable and heartfelt song from the 1994 album "Universal Mother," "Thank You for Hearing Me" showcases Sinead's personal poetry.

6. "Fire on Babylon" (1994) - This song from "Universal Mother" is renowned for its potent social criticism and exemplifies Sinead's drive to confront significant themes in her music.

These band and solo projects are but a sample of Sinead O'Connor's extensive collection of work. Her desire to try new genres and collaborate with diverse artists has enabled her to make a lasting impression on the music industry, and her passionate performances and powerful voice continue to captivate audiences all over the world.

CHAPTER 3: NOTABLE SONGS AND MUSIC VIDEOS

Numerous well-known songs and music videos that have gained notoriety in the music business are hallmarks of Sinead O'Connor's career. Her bold attitude to confronting significant subjects through her work is reflected in these songs and videos, which also highlight how strong her voice are. Here are some of her best-known songs and the music videos that go along with them:

1. The 1990 song "Nothing Compares 2 U"
"Nothing Compares 2 U," unquestionably Sinead O'Connor's most well-known song, is a moving ballad that was first created by Prince. One of the most iconic music videos in music history is the one for this song. The video, which was directed by John Maybury, is a potent visual accompaniment to the song's moving lyrics. It opens with a close-up of Sinead's face, putting her

unfiltered emotions and vulnerability on full display as she sings of lost love.

2. "Troy" (1987):

The song's strong and impassioned lyrics are matched by O'Connor's emotionally charged vocal performance, making "Troy" a memorable piece from Sinead's debut album, "The Lion and the Cobra." Despite the lack of an official music video for "Troy," the song is still a fan favorite and a reminder of her early talent.

3. The 1990 film "The Emperor's New Clothes"

The dramatic song "The Emperor's New Clothes" is another one from the same album as "Nothing Compares 2 U," and it has words that will get you thinking. The accompanying music video, which was made by John Maybury, features Sinead O'Connor in a white dress and sets the song's themes of political and societal disillusionment against scenes of conflict, squalor, and devastation.

4. (1987) "Mandinka"

Sinéad O'Connor

As one of Sinead's debut hits, "Mandinka" contributed to the discovery of her distinctive voice by a larger audience. Her charismatic stage presence and distinctive shaved head are highlighted in the song video, highlighting her gutsy persona and spellbinding performances.

5. The 1994 film "Fire on Babylon"
"Fire on Babylon," a stirring song from her album "Universal Mother," deals with the subject of social injustice. Sinead O'Connor sings amid a barren terrain while being surrounded by images of political upheaval, environmental destruction, and human misery in the accompanying music video, which was directed by John Maybury.

6. (2012): "4th and Vine"
O'Connor's melancholy lyrics and haunting voice are featured in this song from her album "How About I Be Me (and You Be You)?" In the song video, Sinead can be seen strolling around Dublin's streets while thinking

back on her life and experiences as she reflects on her profession and artistic path.

7. 1994's "Thank You for Hearing Me"
Sinead O'Connor's soul-stirring vocals and genuine poetry are on full display in this emotionally charged ballad from the album "Universal Mother". Despite the song's lack of an official music video, its stirring message of thankfulness and vulnerability struck a chord with listeners all around the world.

8. 1990's "The Last Day of Our Acquaintance"
This moving song, which can be found on the album "I Do Not Want What I Haven't Got," explores the complexity of a breaking relationship. Sinead O'Connor performs mesmerizingly in the song's music video, which was created by John Maybury and emphasizes the raw emotions she conveys through her voice and facial gestures against a stark black background.

9. Live Performance of "Take Me to Church" (Hozier Cover)

Sinéad O'Connor

The popular song "Take Me to Church" by Hozier is performed live by Sinead O'Connor, showcasing both of her exceptional vocal abilities and emotional range. Her deep vocal adds a distinct and eerie dimension to the already potent song in this live performance, drawing accolades from both fans and other musicians.

10. (2000)'s "Jealous":
The hymn "Jealous" from her album "Faith and Courage" explores themes of jealously and insecurity. Sinead O'Connor performs the song in the accompanying music video against a stunning visual backdrop, emphasizing the intensity of her feelings and the vigor of the song.

11. The unplugged performance of "Thank You for Hearing Me"
The "Thank You for Hearing Me" acoustic unplugged performance by Sinead O'Connor on MTV's "Unplugged" series highlighted both her extraordinary vocal prowess and the unadulterated intimacy of her song. Without the benefit of a complex staging, her

emotional performance of the song captivated the audience and cemented her image as an engaging live singer who evokes strong emotions.

12. The 1990 song "I Am Stretched on Your Grave"
I Am Stretched on Your Grave" by Sinead O'Connor is a haunting and evocative song from Sinead O'Connor's album "I Do Not Want What I Haven't Got." The music video for the song, which was directed by John Maybury, features O'Connor giving a captivating performance in a surreal and dreamlike setting, adding to the song's mesmerizing and otherworldly atmosphere.

13. (2002)'s "My Darling Child"
"My Darling Child" is a delicate and heartbreaking song from Sinead's album "Sean-Nós Nua," and it highlights her emotive vocal performance. Her frank and open performance is captured in the song's music video, giving listeners an affecting and personal experience.

14. 2012's "Reason with Me"

Sinéad O'Connor

The powerful vocals and open lyrics of Sinead may be heard on this moving song from the album "How About I Be Me (and You Be You)?" A vulnerable and reflective Sinead is portrayed in the music video, which was created by Courtney Love and adds a personal touch to the song's emotional depth.

15. Live at Féile, 1990's "Nothing Compares 2 U"
The live rendition of "Nothing Compares 2 U" by Sinead O'Connor during the 1990 Féile Festival in Ireland is a spellbinding demonstration of her vocal prowess and emotional connection with the crowd. One of the best live performances of the well-known song, the video perfectly captures the unadulterated intensity of her performance.

16. 1995's "The Foggy Dew" (performed by The Chieftains):
In a haunting performance of "The Foggy Dew," Sinead worked with legendary Irish folk group The Chieftains. Her strong vocals combined with traditional Irish music

produce a moving and emotive experience that pays homage to Irish history and legacy.

17. Nirvana Cover of "All Apologies" (2014):
Sinead O'Connor gave a genuine and affecting performance of Nirvana's "All Apologies" as a profound homage to the late Kurt Cobain. Her soulful rendition of the iconic song demonstrated her ability to give new life to great compositions while keeping their emotional essence.

18. 1994's "In This Heart"
"In This Heart" is a soul-stirring song from her album "Universal Mother," with deep lyrics that discuss themes of love, compassion, and oneness. Sinead's captivating performance, which wonderfully complements the song's emotional depth, may be seen in the accompanying music video.

19. (2000)'s "I Believe in You"
The emotional and inspirational song "I Believe in You" is from Sinead's album "Faith and Courage," and it

displays her upbeat and cheerful side. The music video for the song showcases her radiant presence amid symbols of faith and resiliency, highlighting the song's uplifting message.

20. "Whomsoever Dwells" (produced in 2002 with Asian Dub Foundation):
Sinead contributed her vocals to "Whomsoever Dwells" in an original collaboration with the British electronic band Asian Dub Foundation. Her strong voice and the band's edgy and politically charged sound came together to create a fascinating and socially conscious composition.

21. (2011): "The Wolf Is Getting Married"
She reflects on love and commitment in this thought-provoking piece from her album "How About I Be Me (and You Be You)?" In the music video that goes along with the song, Sinead gives a visually arresting performance that captures the emotional complexity and sensitivity of the song.

22. (1998) "This Is a Rebel Song"
Originally published as the B-side to her single "This Is to Mother You," "This Is a Rebel Song" is a strong and rebellious song that deals with problems of oppression and resistance. The song stands out in her record due to Sinead's passionate performance and the heartbreaking lyrics.

23. The 1990 song "Just Like U Said It Would B"
This song, from Sinead's breakthrough album "I Do Not Want What I Haven't Got," demonstrates her talent for expressing sadness and vulnerability through song. The music video effectively captures the emotional intensity of her performance, enhancing the song's evocative lyrics.

24. The 2005 song "I Guess the Lord Must Be in New York City"
In her performance of the Harry Nilsson classic, Sinead gives the song's soulful, introspective lyrics a special touch. A reflective Sinead can be seen strolling the

streets of New York City in the music video, which fits the song's regretful and depressing tone.

25. (2014) "Scarlet Ribbons"

Sinead displays her ethereal and delicate vocals in this lovely rendition of the old folk tune "Scarlet Ribbons." The song's personal spirit is perfectly captured in the music video, giving viewers a gripping and deeply moving experience.

26. (1997) "Tiny Grief Song"

Tiny Grief Song," a moving and thoughtful ballad from her album "Gospel Oak EP," explores themes of loss and recovery. Listeners will have an emotional and intimate experience with the song thanks to the music video, which features Sinead in a private environment and portrays the song's raw passion.

27. (2002)'s "She Moved Through the Fair"

A haunting and ethereal masterpiece from Sinead O'Connor's album "Sean-Nós Nua," "She Moved Through the Fair" is a classic Irish folk ballad, and

Sinead O'Connor's rendition of it is a haunting and ethereal masterpiece.

28. (2004): "My Special Child"

"My Special Child," a touching ode to her son Shane, is taken from her album "She Who Dwells in the Secret Place of the Most High Shall Abide Under the Shadow of the Almighty." The song's emotional impact is further enhanced by the music video, which shows tender moments between a mother and kid.

29. (2002)'s "Paddy's Lament"

"Paddy's Lament" is another excellent song from "Sean-Nós Nua," and it tackles themes of Irish history and immigration. The song's potent narrative is complemented by the music video's historical footage and moving images, which sheds light on the difficulties endured by Irish emigrants.

30. 1994's "The Healing Room"

A lyrical and introspective song from her album "Universal Mother," "The Healing Room" speaks on the need for emotional restoration. The song's themes of vulnerability and self-discovery are given more depth by the video, which captures Sinead O'Connor's unfiltered and visceral performance.

31. 2005's "The Singing Bird"

"The Singing Bird" is one of the songs from her reggae-influenced album "Throw Down Your Arms," and it stands out for its inspirational and spiritually driven message. The song's Jamaican flavor is perfectly encapsulated in the video, displaying Sinead's affinity for the genre's origins.

32. 1997's "When You Love":

The gentle and passionate ballad "When You Love" from the "City of Angels" soundtrack perfectly accompanies the love themes of the movie. The song's emotional effect is increased by Sinead's expressive vocals, making it a standout addition to the soundtrack.

Audiences of all ages continue to connect with Sinead O'Connor's well-known songs and music videos, demonstrating her capacity to communicate unfiltered emotion, vulnerability, and strength via her work. Each song is a distinct phase in her musical journey and reflects her unrelenting commitment to being an honest, trustworthy, and brave artist.

Sinead O'Connor continues to be a symbol of sincerity and passion in the music industry as her tremendous legacy survives, inspiring both fellow musicians and audiences with her timeless contributions to the musical environment. One of the most admired and significant figures in the history of contemporary music, her work continues to transcend boundaries and resonate emotionally with audiences.

CHAPTER 4: CONTROVERSIES AND POLITICAL ACTIVISM

Sinead O'Connor's career has been characterized by controversy and political engagement, which reflects her steadfast dedication to using her platform to confront social concerns and promote causes she is passionate about. She has bravely spoken her opinions on a variety of topics throughout her career, earning praise and condemnation from the general people and the media. Here are some of the major political action issues and controversies involving Sinead O'Connor:

1. The SNL Pope Picture Incident (1992): During Sinead O'Connor's performance on "Saturday Night Live" in 1992, one of the most major conflicts in her career took place. When she had finished singing Bob Marley's "War," she put up a picture of Pope John Paul II and sang the word "evil." After that, she tore the picture to pieces and claimed that she was doing it to protest sexual abuse

in the Catholic Church. Many people were outraged by this behavior, notably religious organizations, which resulted in harsh condemnation and retaliation.

2. Advocacy Against Child Abuse and the Catholic Church: Sinead O'Connor's Catholic upbringing and her stay in a Magdalene Asylum had a significant impact on her advocacy against child abuse and the structural problems in the Catholic Church. She has criticized the Church's handling of abuse cases in an outspoken manner and demanded accountability and justice for victims. Her stance on this subject has received criticism from some religious organizations and conservative groups in addition to support from survivors and those calling for reform.

3. Lyrical Themes and Taboo Subjects: Sinead O'Connor bravely tackled taboo subjects and delved into themes of sexuality, religion, and political unrest throughout her record. Her lyrics frequently included open and occasionally contentious confessions of personal experiences and opinions. Songs like "Black Boys on

Mopeds" and "The Wolf Is Getting Married" addressed problems of racism and same-sex marriage, respectively.

4. Rejecting Awards and Mainstream Recognition: Despite her enormous success and widespread praise, Sinead O'Connor occasionally rejects awards and main stream recognition because she despises the music business's commercial side. Her intention to disassociate herself from what she sees as the industry's exploitation of artists and preference for business over art has been made clear.

5. Political Activism and Social Justice: Sinead O'Connor has been active in a number of political and social justice initiatives in addition to her music. She has advocated for women's rights, LGBTQ+ rights, and the rights of those seeking asylum. In a world beset by myriad social and political issues, her activism has frequently centered on advancing compassion, love, and understanding.

6. Mental Health and Personal Struggles: Sinead O'Connor has been forthright about her battles with mental health conditions, and her candor has inspired talks about mental health awareness in the media. She has advocated for improved recognition of and assistance for persons coping with mental health issues by drawing on her personal experiences.

Sinead O'Connor's political involvement and conflicts have occasionally overshadowed her music, but they have also increased her influence as a well-known person who isn't afraid to utilize her platform for advocacy and change. Her status as a lasting and significant artist who utilizes her voice to make a significant influence on the world as both a singer and an activist has been cemented by her sincerity, boldness, and desire for social justice.

4.1 Pope Picture Incident involving SNL

The SNL Pope Picture Incident, which took place on October 3, 1992, during an edition of "Saturday Night Live," continues to be one of Sinead O'Connor's most pivotal moments. Sinead's protest against sexual abuse in the Catholic Church was the subject of the incident, which attracted a lot of media attention and great debate.

Sinead O'Connor made a strong statement against the church's treatment of child abuse cases during her performance of the song "War," which is based on a speech by Haile Selassie, the former Emperor of Ethiopia. She held up a picture of Pope John Paul II at the conclusion of the song and repeatedly sang the word "evil" before shredding the picture to pieces. "Fight the real enemy," she commanded, alluding to the necessity to deal with the problem of child abuse within the Catholic Church.

The Pope's portrait was torn on live television, shocking the audience and people around. She received harsh criticism for her behavior from the media, religious institutions, and a wide range of public figures. Sinead O'Connor received anger and criticism, and others called for a ban on her future live performances and broadcast appearances.

Her career was badly impacted by the incident's notoriety. Records and radio airplay both significantly decreased as a result, and numerous scheduled television appearances were canceled. Due of the response, some concert venues even declined to host her performances.

However, the event also received backing from a number of organizations and people who admired her boldness in bringing up a difficult and significant matter. Victims' rights activists and survivors of sexual abuse in the Church expressed their appreciation for her position.

Sinead O'Connor has justified her actions throughout the years, claiming that her protest was not against the Catholic faith but rather against the organization's failure to deal with the problem of child abuse within its ranks.

She insisted that her goal was to break the silence and secrecy around the subject while also bringing attention to the situation of abuse victims.

The SNL Pope Picture Incident is still a contentious episode in Sinead O'Connor's life and a topic of controversy and debate in both the music business and the general public. It demonstrates her courage in using her platform to speak out on significant social issues despite the possibility of negative personal and professional consequences.

4.2 The Catholic Church's Child Abuse Protest

One of Sinead O'Connor's main points of activity is her opposition to child abuse in the Catholic Church. She uses her voice and platform to demand accountability and justice from the Church as a result of her personal experiences, Catholic upbringing, and profound care for the victims of abuse.

Sinead O'Connor has firsthand experience with the institutional and cultural problems that have impacted women and children within the Catholic Church because she spent time in a Magdalene Asylum as a young girl. Her commitment to be a strong voice for individuals who have experienced comparable horrors has been strengthened by her own experiences of abuse and neglect.

O'Connor has consistently attacked the Catholic Church for its treatment of child abuse allegations over the course of her career. She has criticized the institution's pervasive inability to defend victims and prosecute offenders. She has pushed for openness, change, and assistance for survivors in interviews, lectures, and other public appearances.

The 1992 SNL Pope Picture Incident (discussed in section 4.1) was one of her most noteworthy campaigns against child abuse in the Church. She wanted to raise awareness of the problem and demand action, so she tore up a picture of Pope John Paul II on live television. The episode not only caused a great deal of criticism and backlash, but it also sparked debates regarding the obligation of religious institutions to deal with abuse inside their ranks.

After that occurrence, Sinead O'Connor continued to support abuse victims by using her music, interviews, and social media. She has advocated for the Catholic Church to take decisive action to safeguard children and support survivors, speaking out against the culture of silence and denial that has allowed abuse to continue.

Many abuse survivors and activists have praised her action and praised her for having the bravery and tenacity to bring attention to a subject that has long been shrouded in secrecy. She has persisted in using her voice for the greater good despite opposition and reaction, regardless of the repercussions for herself.

Sinead O'Connor's demonstration against child abuse in the Catholic Church is a prime example of her unwavering commitment to utilize her platform to advance social justice and significant change. She has been a significant voice in the struggle against abuse and the defense of vulnerable people inside religious organizations as a result of her advocacy, which has helped to advance dialogues about the necessity of responsibility, transparency, and support for survivors.

4.3 Opinions on Spirituality and Religion

Throughout her life and career, Sinead O'Connor's opinions on religion and spirituality have been nuanced and fluid. Her early relationship with religion was significantly influenced by her Irish Catholic upbringing. But as she got older, she developed a new outlook on organized religion and spirituality.

1. Opposition to Organized Religion: Sinead O'Connor has expressed her disapproval of organized religion and the Catholic Church, especially in light of how they have handled matters like child abuse and the treatment of

women. She expressed her displeasure with the Church's hierarchy and structural issues by speaking out against child abuse during the SNL Pope Picture Incident (described in section 4.1).

2. Adopting a Personal Spiritual path: Sinead O'Connor adopted a more individualized and varied spiritual path as she removed herself from institutional religion. She looked at a variety of spiritual practices and beliefs, including parts of Rastafarianism, Paganism, and Christianity. Her interest in many spiritual traditions is a reflection of her yearning to discover meaning outside of traditional religious systems and her quest for a closer relationship with the divine.

3. A Connection to Nature and Celtic Spirituality: Sinead's spirituality has also been affected by her Irish heritage and love of the natural world. She has admitted to having a soft spot for Celtic mysticism, which frequently emphasizes how interconnected all living things are to one another and to the natural world. Her music and public speeches frequently touch on this

relationship with nature and respect for Ireland's old customs.

4. Deep Emotional Connection with God: Sinead O'Connor has remained emotionally and personally connected to God throughout her career, and this is clear in many of her songs. She frequently uses music as a vehicle for her spiritual expression, using it to share her deepest thoughts and emotions about her connection to the divine.

5. Promotion of Love and Compassion: Sinead O'Connor's spirituality has continuously been focused on themes of love, compassion, and empathy, notwithstanding her criticisms of organized religion. She promotes the value of treating everyone with love and understanding, regardless of their views or social circumstances.

Sinead O'Connor has been candid about her battles with mental health concerns, and faith has been a major part of her coping techniques. She has discussed how her spiritual practices, such as prayer and meditation, have been essential in assisting her in maintaining equilibrium and finding calm during trying times.

Sinead O'Connor's perspectives on religion and spirituality are the result of a very introspective journey. Her rejection of organized religion has not lessened her awe of the divine but has instead inspired her to investigate other forms of spirituality. She continues to push for a more open-minded and compassionate understanding of faith and humanity through her activism and music.

4.4 Additional Protest and Advocacy

Sinead O'Connor has participated in numerous additional activism and advocacy initiatives throughout her career in addition to her outspoken opinions on religion and spirituality and her campaigning against child abuse in the Catholic Church. She has addressed a variety of topics as a result of her dedication to social justice and use of her platform for good change. These are some of the various fields she has participated in:

1. LGBTQ+ Rights: Sinead O'Connor has been a vocal supporter of LGBTQ+ rights and has denounced the prejudice and inequity that the LGBTQ+ community must contend with. She has advocated for equality and acceptance of LGBTQ+ people through her music and interviews.

2. Women's Rights: Sinead O'Connor has fought for women's rights and gender equality as a female in the male-dominated music industry. She has promoted gender empowerment and inclusivity while highlighting the difficulties experienced by women in the entertainment industry and society at large.

3. Opposition to war: Throughout her career, O'Connor has been a vocal opponent of violence and war. She has promoted peace and denounced war and military operations using her songs and public platform.

4. Mental Health Awareness: Sinead O'Connor has become a vocal proponent for mental health help and awareness as a result of her experiences with her mental health. She has been transparent about her own struggles with mental illness, which has helped to dispel stigma and increase knowledge of these problems.

5. Support for Refugees and Asylum Seekers: O'Connor has advocated for compassion and support for people who have been uprooted by conflict and persecution. She has been outspoken about the suffering of refugees and asylum seekers.

6. Opposition to Capital Punishment: She has also stated her opposition to the death penalty and has made use of her platform to advocate for its repeal.

7. Environmental Advocacy: Sinead O'Connor is a supporter of sustainability and environmental protection since she loves the outdoors. She has made use of her position to spread knowledge about environmental

concerns and the significance of taking action to safeguard the environment.

8. Anti-Racism Initiatives: Sinead O'Connor has actively opposed racism and pushed for racial equality. Her lyrics and public pronouncements frequently speak to the need for harmony and understanding between people of all racial and ethnic backgrounds.

The hallmark of Sinead O'Connor's activism and advocacy has been her readiness to take on urgent social concerns and use her voice to elevate the voices of underrepresented groups. She has become a strong advocate for love, compassion, and understanding as a result of her unwavering commitment to doing so. She has endured criticism and controversy for her opinions, but she hasn't wavered in her determination to use her activism and music to make a real difference.

CHAPTER 5: PERSONAL STRUGGLE AND MENTAL HEALTH

The difficulties of Sinead O'Connor's personal life and her problems with mental illness have been recurring topics in her work. She has been upfront and honest about her experiences, using her position to push for better understanding and support for individuals dealing with comparable difficulties as well as to raise awareness about mental health issues. The following are some significant facets of her own problems and journey with mental health:

1. Family strife and childhood trauma:
Sinead O'Connor had a challenging and chaotic upbringing. She spoke about the verbal and physical abuse she received from her mother as a child and the difficult familial setting in which she was raised. These early encounters left a lasting impression on her emotional health and sense of self.

2. diagnosis of mental illness

O'Connor has battled different mental health conditions throughout her life, such as bipolar illness, anxiety, and despair. She has been identified as having bipolar disorder, commonly known as manic depression, a mental illness marked by sharp mood swings between manic highs and depressed lows.

3. Hospitalizations and Suicide Attempts:

Sinead O'Connor has been transparent about her history of hospitalizations and suicide attempts. She has experienced extreme emotional suffering as a result of her mental health issues, and she has sought help and treatment to deal with them.

4. Influence on art and music:

Her artistic expression and songs have been profoundly impacted by her personal problems and mental health journey. She explores her emotional anguish, vulnerability, and desire for self-discovery in several of her songs. She has used her music to express her feelings and to connect with people who might be going through similar things.

5. Promoting awareness of mental health issues
Sinead O'Connor's problems with her mental health have inspired her to speak out in favor of mental health care and awareness. She has spoken candidly about her experiences on public platforms, helping to dispel the stigma associated with mental illness and enticing others to get support and treatment.

6. Coping strategies
O'Connor has used a variety of coping strategies to manage her mental health throughout her life, including music, prayer, meditation, and counseling. She has emphasized the value of self-care and discovering healthy strategies to deal with the difficulties associated with mental health.

7. Trying to Get Media Attention:
Media attention and sensationalism have made her mental health issues even more difficult. Her emotional

discomfort has occasionally increased due to the media's focus on her personal life and difficulties, which has impacted her public image.

Sinead O'Connor has overcome numerous obstacles, but her tenacity and resolve to talk honestly about mental health have inspired many. She has broken down boundaries and promoted more understanding and compassion for individuals coping with similar challenges because of her desire to be open about her weaknesses and speak out for mental health awareness.

Even in the face of public scrutiny, Sinead O'Connor's challenges in her personal life and struggles with her mental health serve as an example of why it is crucial to recognize and treat mental health concerns. Her advocacy and singing have powerfully acted as a reminder of the strength that can be discovered in weakness and the therapeutic value of creative expression.

5.1 Struggles with Bipolar Disorder and Depression

Sinead O'Connor has been outspoken about her struggles with bipolar disorder, sometimes known as manic depression, and sadness. Her life and work have been greatly impacted by these mental health issues, which have caused her to experience extreme emotional highs and lows. The following details her encounters with depression and bipolar disorder in further detail:

1. Suffering from depression:
Sinead O'Connor has struggled with depression on numerous occasions during her life. It is a mood illness marked by a loss of interest or pleasure in activities and enduring emotions of despair and pessimism. O'Connor has been candid about her struggles with depression, frequently describing it as a debilitating and isolating condition.

Sinéad O'Connor

2. Bipolar disorder's cyclical nature

A mental health disease known as bipolar disorder is characterized by recurrent episodes of mania (elevated mood and activity) and depression. Intense mood fluctuations caused by Sinead O'Connor's bipolar condition have caused her to experience periods of increased vitality and inventiveness as well as profoundly negative and depressing feelings.

3. Effect on musical career:

O'Connor's struggles with mental illness have had a significant effect on her music and career. She has had difficulties recording and performing when depressed. On the other side, manic episodes have frequently sparked her creativity and resulted in bursts of intense artistic expression and productivity.

4. Disclosure of Suicide Attempts:

Sinead O'Connor has been open about her history of suicide attempts and how her battles with mental illness have driven her to the verge of hopelessness. Her candor regarding these experiences has contributed to de-stigmatizing conversations about suicide and mental illness.

5. Getting Expert Assistance:
O'Connor has sought expert assistance for managing her mental health throughout her life. She has had counseling and various forms of treatment to help stabilize her health while being hospitalized during times that have been extremely trying.

6. Drugs and coping mechanisms:
Sinéad O'Connor has utilized medicine to control her bipolar condition and to balance her moods. She has also used coping mechanisms including prayer, meditation, and creative expression to get over the challenges of her mental health.

7. Awareness of mental health issues and advocacy
Due to her own struggles with depression and bipolar disorder, Sinead O'Connor has decided to promote mental health awareness. She inspires others to get assistance, lowers stigma, and promotes knowledge of

mental health concerns through her candor and advocacy.

8. Relationships and public perception are affected:
Her struggles with bipolar disorder and depression have also had an effect on her relationships and public image. Her public image has been impacted by media scrutiny and sensationalization of her issues, which has occasionally led to misconceptions regarding her mental health.

The experience of Sinead O'Connor with depression and bipolar disorder serves as a powerful reminder of the value of raising awareness about mental health issues, eliminating stigma, and getting assistance when needed. Many people who may be coping with similar problems have benefited from her candor about her experiences, showing that being vulnerable and asking for help may make a significant difference in the healing process.

5.2 Effect on Career and Music

The struggles Sinead O'Connor has faced with bipolar disorder and depression have had a significant impact on her music and career. Her artistic expression and public persona have been impacted by these mental health issues in terms of themes, intensity, and trajectory. The following are some ways that her battles with mental illness have influenced her music and career:

1. Music that is introspective and evocative:
O'Connor's music is intensely emotional and introspective as a result of her personal experiences with depression and bipolar disease. Her emotional difficulties, frailties, and quest for purpose are frequently reflected in her music. She has been able to express her feelings and engage audiences deeply through her songs.

2. Outbursts of creativity and productivity
Sinead O'Connor has experienced spurts of inspiration and increased energy when going through her manic stages of bipolar disease. There has frequently been a

spike in songwriting and recording at these times. Her career has consequently experienced bursts of high productivity and creative creativity.

3. Performances at concerts:
O'Connor's struggles with her mental health have occasionally interfered with her live performances. She has occasionally had to postpone or cancel performances because of her emotional health. On the other hand, she has given strong and impassioned live performances when frenzied.

4. Authenticity and Vulnerability
Sinead O'Connor's public presence now has a touch more sensitivity and sincerity because to her desire to be upfront about her battles with depression and bipolar disorder. Fans have responded well to her candor about her mental health, which has helped to humanize her in the public view.

5. Misperceptions about the media

Sinéad O'Connor

Her struggles with mental illness have received a lot of media attention, which has occasionally resulted in misunderstandings and sensationalism. Her hardships have occasionally overshadowed her artistic accomplishments in the public, which has resulted in undue examination of her personal life.

6. Impact on the Release of Albums:
O'Connor's struggles with her mental health have occasionally affected when her albums were released. Her musical endeavors have been delayed by times of emotional upheaval or instability, which has affected the scheduling of record releases.

7. Promoting awareness of mental health issues
O'Connor has developed into an outspoken supporter of mental health awareness and education as a result of her personal struggles with mental illness. Her advocacy has aided in eradicating stigmas associated with mental illness and inspired others to seek care.

8. Individual Development and Resilience:

Sinéad O'Connor

Sinead O'Connor has shown amazing persistence and tenacity in her career despite the obstacles presented by her mental health issues. Her resilience in the face of adversity has demonstrated her development as a person and an artist, as well as her strength.

Sinead O'Connor's battle with mental illness has had a significant impact on her music and career. She has had a lasting influence on the music industry and how people view mental health issues thanks to her candor about her struggles, her artistic expression of emotion, and her advocacy for mental health awareness. She has thereby established herself as not just a powerful artist but also a role model in the fight against stigma surrounding mental illness and a supporter of more understanding and assistance for people dealing with comparable difficulties.

CHAPTER 6: COLLABORATION WITH OTHER ARTISTS

Collaborations between Sinead O'Connor and other musicians have been a crucial aspect of her artistic path, displaying her adaptability and capacity to fit in with a variety of musical styles. The following major partnerships have enhanced her discography:

1. U2 and "I'm Not Your Baby" from 1995:
Sinead O'Connor and Bono's stirring duet "I'm Not Your Baby" is included on the soundtrack for the movie "The End of the Violence." O'Connor's deep vocals and Bono's distinctive voice are expertly paired throughout the song to create a haunting and intense track.

2. (2003)'s "Special Cases" featuring Massive Attack
On the song "Special Cases," which she co-wrote with the renowned trip-hop group Massive Attack, Sinead O'Connor's ethereal vocals and the band's atmospheric

sound combine to create a hypnotic and thought-provoking composition that explores issues of abuse and violence.

3. (2008)'s "Haunted" starring Shane MacGowan:
For the tender duet "Haunted," Sinead O'Connor teamed up with Shane MacGowan, the illustrious frontman of The Pogues. Their voices blend well, giving a heartbreaking and melancholy tune that demonstrates their emotional range as singers.

4. 1989's "Kingdom of Rain" featuring The The
Sinead O'Connor works with the English alternative band The The on the song "Kingdom of Rain." The melancholy and ominous song shows O'Connor's variety of emotional expression, making it a standout addition to both artists' discographies.

5. Afro Celt Sound System's "Release" in 1999:
Sinead O'Connor gives her fascinating voice to "Release" in this engaging collaboration with the Afro Celt Sound System. The song mixes traditional Irish

components with electronic and world music influences, creating a strong and hypnotic musical experience.

6. Gavin Friday and Maurice Seezer's "You Made Me the Thief of Your Heart" (1994):

Sinead O'Connor, Gavin Friday, and Maurice Seezer created "You Made Me the Thief of Your Heart" as part of the soundtrack for the movie "In the Name of the Father," which brilliantly reflects the emotional depth of the film's themes.

7. With The Edge, they sang "Don't Cry for Me Argentina" in 1996.

For a special performance of "Don't Cry for Me Argentina" from the musical "Evita," Sinead O'Connor and U2's guitarist, The Edge, teamed up. Their rendition gives the classic song a new, emotional perspective.

These projects not only reflect Sinead O'Connor's superb vocal ability but also her desire to experiment with many musical styles and collaborate with a wide range of musicians. She continually adds her special touch to every project she works on in partnership, making a lasting imprint on both the music and her audiences. Her collaborations with other musicians have expanded her artistic palette and strengthened her position as a renowned and prominent figure in the music business.

6.1 Composing and composing songs for other musicians

Sinead O'Connor has made substantial contributions as a lyricist and composer for other musicians, yet she is best known for her passionate performances and powerful vocals. Her musical abilities and beautiful, contemplative lyrics have led to a number of fruitful partnerships with other musicians. Examples of Sinead O'Connor's songwriting and composition work for other artists include the following:

1. Linda Ronstadt (1995): "This Is to Mother You" (co-written with Glen Ballard and Eric Bazilian):

Sinéad O'Connor

The heartfelt song "This Is to Mother You" was
co-written by Sinead O'Connor, Glen Ballard, and Eric
Bazilian. The song was written and performed by Linda
Ronstadt for her album "Feels Like Home." Its
sentimental lyrics and emotional delivery are resonant
with ideas of parental support and affection.

2. Asian Dub Foundation with Sinead O'Connor, "1000
Mirrors" (co-written with DJ Krush and Michael Franti,
2003):
Sinead O'Connor worked on "1000 Mirrors," a stirring
song by the Asian Dub Foundation, with DJ Krush and
Michael Franti. The song incorporates trip-hop, reggae,
and electronica sounds, while O'Connor offers her
distinctive vocals to address themes of introspection and
atonement.

3. "Empire" by Bomb the Bass ft. Sinead O'Connor
(1994) (co-written with Brian Eno):
For the song "Empire," Sinead O'Connor collaborated
with Bomb the Bass and Brian Eno. O'Connor's ethereal
vocals give the electronic track—which she co-wrote

with renowned producer Brian Eno—an atmospheric and eerie feel.

4. (2003) song "Harbour" by Mundy with Sinead O'Connor:
For the song "Harbour," which includes O'Connor singing the chorus and showcasing her emotive voice, Sinead O'Connor collaborated with Irish singer-songwriter Mundy.

5. "The Wolf Is Getting Married" by Sinéad O'Connor, from The Gloaming, was released in 2012:
The hauntingly gorgeous song "The Wolf Is Getting Married," written by Sinead O'Connor, explores themes of love and change. She sang it on her album "How About I Be Me (And You Be You)?," and the Irish-American ensemble The Gloaming later covered it for their self-titled album.

6. The 1995 song "I Can't Stop Thinking About You" by Sinéad O'Connor:

Sinéad O'Connor

Sinead O'Connor wrote and produced the song "I Can't Stop Thinking About You" for her album "Universal Mother." The song showcases her introspective and emotionally charged lyrics that focus on themes of love and longing.

7. Sinéad O'Connor's song "Dagger Through the Heart" was released in 2012:
For her album "How About I Be Me (And You Be You)," Sinead O'Connor penned and composed the song "Dagger Through the Heart," which highlights her honest and sincere expression of love and vulnerability.

8. 2012's "Something Beautiful" by Sinéad O'Connor:
"Something Beautiful" is a song that addresses themes of self-discovery and discovering beauty inside oneself. It was written and recorded by Sinead O'Connor. Her album "How About I Be Me (And You Be You)?" contains the song.

9. Sinéad O'Connor's "Dark I Am Yet Lovely" (2014):

Sinéad O'Connor

The album "Songs of Ascent" was created in collaboration with several musicians, including Sinead O'Connor. She composed and performed the song "Dark I Am Yet Lovely" for this production, which combines Irish folklore and spiritual themes.

10. Sinéad O'Connor's "Take Off Your Shoes" (2014): Another song written and recorded by Sinead O'Connor is "Take Off Your Shoes," which is also included on the album "Songs of Ascent." O'Connor's captivating vocals and the song's reflective lyrics provide listeners a soul-stirring experience.

11. Sinéad O'Connor's "Out of the Depths" (2019): The extremely personal and emotional album "No Mud No Lotus," which Sinead O'Connor published in 2019, was entirely written and composed by the singer-songwriter. One of the songs that highlights her profound lyrical and emotive delivery is "Out of the Depths".

Sinéad O'Connor

The songwriting and composition work Sinead O'Connor has done for other musicians reflects her beautiful lyrics, thought-provoking ideas, and capacity to genuinely engage audiences. She has been able to share her musical vision and creative abilities with a larger audience through these collaborations, and she has had a lasting influence on the songs she has contributed to. Her collaborations demonstrate her flexibility as a musician and an artist, adding to the diverse body of music that she has introduced to the world.

CHAPTER 7: AWARDS AND RECOGNITION

Sinead O'Connor is a very well-known and significant musician who has won honors and recognition for her extraordinary talent and contributions to the music business. She has won numerous honors and awards, some of which include:

1. Sinead O'Connor has received numerous Grammy Award nominations during the course of her career. She received the Grammy Award in 1991 for "I Do Not Want What I Haven't Got," the album that featured her well-known single "Nothing Compares 2 U.", for Best Alternative Music Performance.

2. MTV Video Music Awards: She received three nominations for her music video for "Nothing Compares 2 U" at the 1990 MTV Video Music Awards, winning in the categories of Best Female Video and Video of the Year.

Sinéad O'Connor

3. The prestigious Brit Award for Best International Female Solo Artist was given to O'Connor in 1991.

4. Irish Music Awards: She has received numerous Irish Music Awards in her own Ireland in honor of her contributions to Irish music and culture.

5. Sinead O'Connor was included on VH1's list of the 100 Greatest Women in Rock in 1999, recognizing her contribution and influence on the rock genre.

6. Induction into the Irish Music Hall of Fame: In recognition of her noteworthy contributions to the music industry, she was admitted into the Irish Music Hall of Fame in 2017.

7. O'Connor has been nominated for a Q Award, which honors excellent achievements to the music industry.

8. She has been nominated for the prestigious Meteor Music Awards in Ireland (now known as the Choice Music Prize).

These honors and accolades are proof of Sinead O'Connor's extraordinary talent as a performer, songwriter, and vocalist. She is a renowned personality in the music industry thanks to her expressive and strong voice, as well as her desire to confront significant social topics in her music. Her musical accomplishments and impact on the business have cemented her position as a legendary and important musician, despite the controversy and difficulties her career has also encountered.

7.1 Grammy Awards

Numerous Grammy Award nominations and one victory during her career were evidence of Sinead O'Connor's influence on the music business. The specifics of her Grammy Awards are as follows:

1. Wins of Grammy Awards:
- 1991: "I Do Not Want What I Haven't Got" won the award for "Best Alternative Music Performance."

2. Nominations for Grammy Awards:

- 1991: "Nothing Compares 2 U" was named Record of the Year.

- 1991: "Nothing Compares 2 U" won Song of the Year.

- 1991: "Nothing Compares 2 U" won for best female pop vocal performance.

- 1991: "I Do Not Want What I Haven't Got" won Album of the Year.

A pivotal moment in her career was when she received the Best Alternative Music Performance Grammy Award in 1991. The legendary track "Nothing Compares 2 U," which went on to become a huge global smash and is now one of her most well-known songs, was featured on the album "I Do Not Want What I Haven't Got," which was released in 1990.

She received nominations for Record of the Year, Song of the Year, and Best Female Pop Vocal Performance for "Nothing Compares 2 U," which was a strong and moving performance. Her standing as a notable performer in the music business was further enhanced by the song's intensely moving music video, which further contributed to its success.

Sinead O'Connor's status as one of the most important musicians of her day was further cemented by the album "I Do Not Want What I Haven't Got" being nominated for Album of the Year.

Even though Sinead O'Connor earned a lot of attention from the Grammy Awards during this time, it's crucial to remember that her effect on the music business goes far beyond award shows. Her unflinchingly honest approach to music and her courage in tackling delicate and thought-provoking subjects have made a lasting impression on both the music industry and the cultural environment.

7.2 Brit Awards

Sinead O'Connor's achievements to the music industry have also been honored by the British Phonographic Industry's annual Brit Awards. The specifics of her Brit Award are as follows:

Best International Female Solo Artist in 1991

The coveted Brit Award for Best International Female Solo Artist was given to Sinead O'Connor in 1991. This honor was a monument to her widespread recognition and the enormous contribution she made with her music, both in the UK and all across the world.

The critically acclaimed album "I Do Not Want What I Haven't Got," which included her timeless hit single "Nothing Compares 2 U," was released in 1991, making it a particularly significant year for O'Connor. It propelled her to international fame and earned her nominations and awards at various ceremonies,

Sinéad O'Connor

including the Grammy Awards and MTV Video Music
Awards.

Sinead O'Connor's position as a notable and
well-respected performer on the global music scene was
cemented by her Brit Award victory for Best
International Female Solo Artist. Her strong vocals,
moving performances, and insightful lyrics struck a
chord with listeners and her contemporaries in the music
business, giving her much-deserved praise.

Beyond the awards, Sinead O'Connor's influence and
legacy as a groundbreaking musician live on in her
timeless music and her bold use of her platform to
promote social justice, mental health awareness, and
other vital causes. Fans and music lovers all across the
world continue to appreciate her contribution to the
music industry and legacy as a significant musician.

CHAPTER 8: LEGACY AND IMPACT

Significant and durable are Sinead O'Connor's impact and influence on the music business. She has made an enduring impact on music and culture as an artist thanks to her emotive depth, strong voice, and courage in tackling touchy subjects. Here are some significant facets of her legacy and impact:

1. Iconic Vocal Style: Sinead O'Connor stands out as one of the most recognizable voices in music thanks to her individual and passionate vocal delivery. She is a mesmerizing artist because to her capacity to transmit unadulterated passion and vulnerability via song.

2. Breakthrough Hit: "Nothing Compares 2 U," a Prince and O'Connor composition that went viral worldwide, is still one of the most recognizable and enduring songs of the 1990s. The song's success propelled her to international notoriety and made her a prominent presence in contemporary music.

3. Honest and Fearless Expression: Throughout her career, Sinead O'Connor bravely used her songs to highlight significant social and political topics. She addressed issues including violence against women, religion, and war, utilizing her platform to promote reform and stimulate discussion.

4. Influence on Female Artists: O'Connor pioneered the road for many female artists to express themselves honestly and question social standards through their music with her audacity and uncompromising honesty. She exemplified how artists can utilize their voices to raise awareness of crucial social issues and have an influence.

5. Crossing Musical Genres: O'Connor's openness to trying out several musical styles, including rock, folk, and electronic, demonstrated her versatility as a musician. She has influenced a generation of musicians looking to push boundaries and discover new aural

realms with her ability to smoothly meld various musical genres.

6. Mental Health Advocacy: Sinead O'Connor has contributed to the reduction of stigma associated with mental health conditions by openly disclosing her battles with depression and bipolar illness. Her advocacy has sparked discussions about mental wellbeing and prompted others to look for help and understanding.

7. O'Connor's enthusiasm for her Irish roots and the way she incorporated traditional Irish components into her music have had a positive impact on the preservation and enjoyment of Irish musical history. She has become as a cultural and musical icon for Ireland.

8. Social activism: In addition to her music, O'Connor has become a symbol of advocacy and sticking up for what she believes in. Her influence has grown outside the music industry as a result of her rallies against social injustice and her outspoken support for neglected populations.

9. Persistent Relevance: Over the years, Sinead O'Connor's music and messages have continued to be influential and relevant. As fresh generations of fans continue to connect with her songs, she is recognized as a timeless artist.

In conclusion, Sinead O'Connor left behind a legacy that is distinguished by her unshakable dedication to truthfulness, social justice, and artistic integrity. Her contributions to music and culture have had a lasting impression and inspired both other artists and activists. She has exceeded the conventional boundaries of the music industry with her strong voice and daring position, leaving a significant and long-lasting mark on society as a whole.

7.1 Effect on Artistic Expression and Music

The influence of Sinead O'Connor on music and artistic expression has been profound and extensive. She transformed the way musicians approach their craft by openly embracing vulnerability and broaching delicate subjects. She has the following major effects on music and aesthetic expression:

1. Honest and Emotional Songwriting: Sinead O'Connor writes songs that are very emotional and deeply personal. She showed how vulnerability and genuineness in music can have a tremendous impact on listeners through her frank and insightful lyrics. She paved the way for other musicians to do the same by being willing to reveal their own challenges and experiences in their songs, which increased the focus on emotional storytelling in music.

2. O'Connor challenged the conventional gender standards in the music industry. She broadened the idea

of gender and womanhood in music by challenging conventions with her shaved head and androgynous appearance. Her daring decisions inspired other female artists to embrace their uniqueness and defy social norms.

3. Fearless Social Commentary: Through her music, Sinead O'Connor boldly addressed social and political issues. She addressed problems like abuse, women's rights, religion, and war using her platform, igniting crucial discussions about these matters. Her artistic involvement served as a demonstration of the potency of music as a tool for social change.

4. Genre blending and versatility: O'Connor's openness to experimenting with several musical genres, from rock to folk to electronic, demonstrated her breadth of artistic expression. She defied genre conventions by fusing many styles and developing a sound all her own. Artists have been motivated by this strategy to investigate various musical influences and produce genre-defying pieces.

5. Influence on Female Artists: Sinead O'Connor's outspoken activism and musical style have served as an inspiration to a great number of female artists. She paved the path for other female musicians to speak up and have an influence in the heavily male-dominated music industry by demonstrating that women could be powerful, vocal, and genuine in their craft.

6. Impact on Mental Health Discourse: By being open about her mental health issues, O'Connor has significantly lessened the stigma associated with mental illness. Her candor has inspired others to ask for assistance, share their stories, and fight for a better understanding of mental health issues.

7. Persistent Relevance: Sinead O'Connor's music continues to speak to younger audiences. Nothing Compares 2 U, her signature hit, continues to be a timeless and well-known song, demonstrating the lasting importance of her work and its capacity to appeal to people throughout time and cultures.

Beyond her financial success and critical recognition, Sinead O'Connor has had a significant impact on music and artistic expression. Her capacity to communicate effectively through her art, touching people's hearts and igniting change, is what gives her impact. She has irrevocably changed the music business, paving the way for musicians to be honest to themselves and speak out on pressing social and emotional concerns.

7.2 Political and Social Influence

As impressive as her musical impact is, Sinead O'Connor also had a significant social and political impact. Throughout her career, she bravely spoke out on significant political topics, fought for social justice, and confronted repressive regimes. Some significant facets of her social and political influence are listed below:

1. Protests Against Child Abuse in the Catholic Church: O'Connor's memorable protest during a live episode of

Sinéad O'Connor

"Saturday Night Live" in 1992 is considered to be one of the most crucial milestones in her social action career. As she sang Bob Marley's "War," which she modified to address child abuse within the Catholic Church, she tore up a picture of Pope John Paul II. The protest sparked debate and discussion regarding the topic of institutional cover-ups and abuse.

2. O'Connor has been a vocal supporter of women's rights, speaking out against topics including domestic abuse, gender inequity, and the right to abortion. Many people have been motivated to speak out against sexism and misogyny as a result of her openness and unabashed feminism.

3. Sinead O'Connor has been a steadfast supporter of the LGBTQ+ community, utilizing her position to speak out against prejudice and advance LGBTQ+ rights. Numerous members of the community have found solace and affirmation in her advocacy.

4. Opposition to War and Violence: O'Connor has repeatedly voiced her opposition to war and violence through her music and activism. By frequently utilizing her art to highlight the human cost of wars and the significance of finding peaceful solutions, she has advocated for peace and understanding.

5. Mental Health Awareness: O'Connor has contributed to lowering the stigma associated with mental illness by being honest about her battles with mental health issues like depression and bipolar disorder. Her campaign has inspired others to ask for treatment, share their stories, and generate more understanding and support for people who are struggling with mental health issues.

6. Standing Up Against Injustice: Sinead O'Connor has never been afraid to speak out against things she considers to be repressive or unjust. She has become a representative of resistance and activism because of her boldness in taking on powerful institutions and fighting for the underprivileged.

7. Music as a Change-Making Tool: O'Connor's songs have been used as anthems for social change, connecting with listeners who share her passion for a world that is more compassionate and just. Her work has inspired viewers to take an active role in pressing social and political concerns.

8. Impact on the World: O'Connor's influence extends well beyond her own Ireland. Her advocacy and music have had a profound impact on listeners all around the world, making her a well-known presence on the global stage.

The social and political impact of Sinead O'Connor emphasizes how artists may use their voices to affect change and advance compassion and understanding. She has continually shown the benefits of using art as a voice for activism, encouraging people to use their own platforms for creativity to defend the principles they hold dear. Numerous people are still motivated by her legacy as a socially conscious and fearless artist to challenge the existing quo and fight towards a more inclusive and just society.

7.3 The Influence on Modern Artists

The impact of Sinead O'Connor on modern artists cuts across a range of artistic expressions and disciplines. A new generation of musicians and activists have been inspired by her daring approach to music, activism for social justice, and openness to tackle sensitive and difficult issues. Here are a few examples of how she has affected modern artists:

1. Emphasis on Authenticity: Sinead O'Connor's dedication to putting true self-expression above adhering to industry standards has affected many contemporary artists. Her willingness to be open about her flaws and challenges has inspired others to follow suit, resulting in more open and relatable music.

2. utilizing Her Platform to Address Social and Political Issues: O'Connor's audacity in utilizing her platform to speak out on social and political issues has encouraged modern artists to get more involved in society and speak out for vital causes. Today, a lot of musicians use their popularity and songs to promote issues like LGBTQ+ rights, gender equality, and human rights.

3. Openness Regarding Mental Health: O'Connor's support of mental health awareness has had a significant influence on modern artists, who now feel more confident to publicly express their own mental health difficulties. Her openness has lessened the stigma associated with mental illness and created a welcoming environment where artists may ask for assistance and support.

4. Music that transcends genres: Sinead O'Connor's openness to experimenting with various musical genres and her genre-defying attitude have influenced modern artists to push boundaries and produce more diverse and avant-garde sounds. Her bravery in fusing genres has

inspired musicians to venture into uncharted aural realms.

5. Feminist Icon: O'Connor is regarded as a feminist icon by many modern artists due to her outspoken feminism and her refusal to follow conventional gender conventions. A new generation of musicians are still affected by her contributions to gender equality and female empowerment.

6. Sinead O'Connor's steadfast dedication to artistic integrity has served as a standard for modern artists. Others have been motivated to be true to themselves and their creative instincts by her refusal to compromise her convictions or artistic vision.

7. Use of Music for Social Change: O'Connor's use of music as a tool for social change has inspired contemporary artists to see their art as a means to raise awareness and promote positive social impact. She set the example for many singers today who use their platforms for activism and advocacy.

Sinéad O'Connor

8. Sinead O'Connor is known for her memorable and passionate vocals, which have had a lasting influence on modern musicians. Her passionate delivery and vocal style continue to have an impact on and inspire vocalists to find their own distinctive voices and establish deeper connections with listeners.

The artistic and activist legacy of Sinead O'Connor has had a profound impact on modern music. She has served as an inspiration for a new generation of artists who want to use their music and activism to improve the world via their bravery, authenticity, and commitment to using their work for good. Her impact is still felt throughout the music industry and beyond as a result.

CONCLUSION

The book "Sinead O'Connor: Unraveling the Soul of a Fearless Artist" explores the life, work, and legacy of one of the most important and recognizable artists of the modern era. We have looked at the incredible journey of a courageous and unapologetic artist who bravely defied norms, exposed her flaws, and used her voice as a potent force for change throughout the pages of this book.

The legacy of Sinead O'Connor is evidence of the potency of honesty and authenticity in song. Her evocative singing, creative composition, and willingness to tackle delicate and socially significant issues have struck a chord with listeners all around the world.

O'Connor has continuously pushed boundaries, encouraging a generation of musicians to embrace their identity and make music with purpose and passion. This is evident in everything from her breakthrough song

Sinéad O'Connor

"Nothing Compares 2 U" to her genre-fusing artistic discoveries.

Sinead O'Connor has had a significant influence on social and political discourse in addition to her musical skills. She has established herself as a representative of activism and resistance because of her bold support of women's rights, LGBTQ+ rights, mental health awareness, and unwavering opposition to injustice and violence.

Her determination to take on established institutions and deal with urgent problems head-on is a testament to the transformative power of art as a force for change.

We have experienced Sinead O'Connor's highs and lows and seen her unwavering dedication to authenticity, artistic integrity, and social duty. While her ground-breaking protest on "Saturday Night Live" continues to inspire talks about child abuse and institutional accountability, her open discussions about mental health difficulties have helped remove stigma and encourage understanding.

Since Sinead O'Connor initially came to prominence, her music has remained both current and influential, and her influence cuts across generations. Artists and activists alike continue to be inspired by her boldness in embracing her true self and utilizing her art to enlighten and empower others.

Her artistic legacy has had a lasting impact on the music business and the larger cultural scene, influencing how we view music, social issues, and self-expression.

In "Sinead O'Connor: Unraveling the Soul of a Fearless Artist," we have found the essence of a visionary musician who dared to be unique, pushed the boundaries, and put her heart and soul into every note she sang. Sinead O'Connor has improved our lives through her music and activism, and she has also left us with a lasting legacy that inspires us to all embrace our

Sinéad O'Connor

individuality, speak our truths, and use our voices to change the world.

Her journey stands as a tribute to the enduring power of art and the ability of a daring artist to touch hearts, elicit thought, and bring about significant social change.

Made in United States
Troutdale, OR
09/30/2023

13309826R00060